FEATHERS 1,2,3:
Essays on Nature and Animals

by Ramnath Subramanian

For my wife, Maria Subramanian,
editor par excellence,
who is the love of my life,
and the source of my daily inspiration

Feathers 1,2,3: Essays on Nature and Animals
Copyright © Ramnath Subramanian, 2021
ISBN: 978-1716231384

Life's Lessons From A Grackle's Visit To The Backyard

The shape in the birdbath was puzzling. Was it a grackle? If so, why did it look so flat?

I opened the french window and stepped outside.

The shape raised itself, — yes, it was a grackle — and took a sip of water.

Then, sensing my presence, it rose to its full height, spread its wings, and half flew, half stumbled out of the birdbath and disappeared behind the lemon tree.

Something was wrong, and I withdrew to give the bird its space.

A few minutes later I went outside to see if the grackle was still there, and found its inert body behind the lemon tree.

I don't know what else I could have done under the circumstances, but I am grateful that the birdbath in our backyard provided the grackle its last sip of water.

This is how life is, I thought to myself. You never know how or when the last curtain will come down. All you can hope for is that the last minutes have some level of comfort to them.

I had never paid too much attention to the grackle.

I looked up to the sky when the hawks were in flight, and it was my wont to stop yard work to listen to the mockingbird's morning symphonies. I also took delight in the hummingbird's gambol.

But the grackle came to my backyard without ceremony, and left without praise.

If there was a Milton in his voice, I never heard it; and if there was a Cromwell in his bravado, I never saw it.

In my writings over the years, the grackle made only one appearance when I compared it in flight to Cleopatra's barge.

In "The Carnival of the Animals" Saint-Saenz included the swan, but not a grackle.

In paintings, too, the main thrust of the brush is on birds with colorful plumage, such as a peacock or a rosella. The artist gives short shrift to the grackle.

However, in "The Elegy Written in a Country Churchyard," Thomas Gray told us that "the boast of heraldry, the pomp of power, and all that beauty and all that wealth e'er gave," amounted to naught in the end.

In a draught-stricken place in India, I recently saw on video women descend the 80-foot wall of a well to scoop up water from a small puddle at the bottom.

They took to the task like Napoleon to the battlefield, but I heard no fife and drums when they emerged victorious from the deep hole, each clutching a plastic bottle filled with dirty water.

In Federico Fellini's movie "La Strada," it is the Fool, an itinerant tightrope walker — and not a personage of standing or stature — who becomes Gelsomina's savior.

Gelsomina is a gentle, simple-minded woman on the cusp of despair, and the Fool confers self-esteem on her by pointing out that even a pebble that exists anonymously has a purpose in life.

The Fool is not dressed in a robe and there are no books at his side, but it is by his words alone that sunshine penetrates the dark clouds in Gelsomina's mind.

After watching the movie, my wife Maria said to me, "It is extraordinary, is it not, that a fool's words, spoken off the cuff, were more life-affirming than anything else Gelsomina had experienced in her entire life."

A hawk in flight may epitomize grandeur, and a mockingbird may be nature's Mozart, but a grackle yet may wear a crown at the propitious hour.

Behind the lemon tree where the grackle lay down its head, I placed four pebbles to represent the points of a compass, and said a small prayer.

The Job Of Education Is To Instill Wonder In Students' Minds

The job of education is not just to teach students how things work, and why things are the way they are, but also to fill their minds with wonder.

Their minds must be made to travel beyond numbers and calculations, hypotheses and proofs, cause and effect, and the whirligig of time, to speculate, contemplate, and meditate on the diverse phenomena of the world that are replete with mysteries and miracles.

Whether studying the symbiotic relationship between a mimosa tree and the beetle that lives on its branches, or probing the plane and ellipticity of orbit that makes life possible on earth, the sui generis lesson should go beyond being a vehicle for information and make the heart sing.

In Thomas Carlyle's "Sartor Resartus," Professor Diogenes Teufelsdrockh summed up these sentiments best, when he said: "The man who cannot wonder, who does not habitually wonder (and worship), were he President of innumerable Royal Societies, and carried the whole Mecanique Celeste and Hagel's Philosophy, and the epitome of all the Laboratories and Observatories with their results in his single head, — is but a Pair of Spectacles behind which there is no Eye."

Is it not a wonder that the bluebonnet puts on a big bright white eye to attract bees to its bosom, but as the florets age dims the signal for the bees?

Is not the Fibonacci sequence of numbers full of mystery?

Isn't it a wonder that the solid phase of water is less dense than its liquid phase (not common for substances), thus allowing it to rise to the surface of ponds and lakes to insulate the lower layers so aquatic life can survive in winter?

The point Professor Teufelsdrockh makes is that we must study everything with celebratory eyes, so that the hand that bends down to pick up the evidence is also the hand that is raised when singing hosannas.

When I was teaching, two or three times in each academic year, I would take my students to an adjacent park for a writing assignment.

I would ask my students to stretch out on the grass or sit leaning against the trunks of trees and jot down a few sentences about things in nature that absolutely amazed them.

I got very many interesting questions and comments.

"What keeps a cloud together?" mused one boy.

A girl said that she would like to study all the nests that different birds build to see which bird was the best architect.

Another girl wanted to know why she felt dizzy looking at the sky when clouds were passing overhead.

"The most amazing thing to me," wrote a boy, "is that there is a sky."

Later, in the classroom, we discussed the observations that had been made, and tried to answer some of the questions.

What is absolutely amazing to me is that from something as infinitesimally small as a zygote, a mind is born that can tackle the universe, write epic poems, and build sky-reaching cathedrals; or brave extraordinary difficulties and obstacles to make grand discoveries.

In short, man himself is a wonder.

I have no doubt that we must reach this plateau of wonder to gain a true appreciation for all the things in life.

Therefore, as teachers, we should expose students to the music that resides in all things, so that an ant colony becomes as prodigious a source of wonder as the mechanics of technology that stream airplanes in and out of airports.

Let us study the acoustics of wind instruments, while a mockingbird regales us with a symphony from a nearby treetop.

The School Of Nature Serves Everyone Well

I met him at the top of Mountain Lake Trail. The air was aromatic with eucalyptus, and yellow-rumped warblers filled the foliage with song. In the clear blue waters of the bay, a brown barge moved softly like poetry.

We stood in the shadow of our silence for a while, and then the man said, "If you stand here long enough, the murmur among the leaves will write your biography."

"Ah, yes," I said, and not knowing what else to add, settled for the prosaic, "such a lovely view from here."

"They must teach children to draw a cloud before they teach them to add and subtract," the man soliloquized.

I reflected on this. During my teaching years I knew many classrooms that had a proclivity to erupt into disorder as soon as the teacher's attention was turned away by some unscheduled occurrence. I wondered if training in nature appreciation and art could condition children's minds to lean toward respect and erudition.

Youngsters today have short attention spans, and I wondered, too, if training in the fine arts could teach children to be more receptive to precious moments.

My introspection was interrupted by the man's speech. "I knew a composer in my youth who told me that bird songs played a large part in his compositions. He would walk softly on these trails, stop frequently, and look up to hear the warbler's slow, soft, sweetly whistled trill. He would chase the songs from tree to tree to the point of satiation."

He stopped for a while lost in thought, and continued: "Today the world is too noisy, and children are trapped in the ruckus. They will have to walk many miles to get to a bird's song."

At this juncture, the man pulled out a piece of folded paper from his jacket pocket, straightened out its creases, and began to read from it:

"If I knew the sweep of winged things — the warbler among the eucalyptus, the egret in the marsh — I would know everything the hawk knows about the earth's fine geometry, and its handsome curvature."

"You see," he said, directing his speech at me for the first time, "we talk a lot about the earth these days, but we would do better to talk about the insidious, modern noise, and how to dispel it.

The weight of noise has turned the earth into just an idea. We no longer feel things, hear things, but talk about them in the abstract.

"Who sees the worm that comes out to greet the rain, or the caterpillar that has its cheek on beauty?

"We have allowed the earth to melt into oblivion. We do not see the quick scamper of a squirrel to the tree top, or the gazelle's walk among the sounds in the forest. We've lost the earth; and we're losing God."

"Will the crooked be made straight again, and the rough way made smooth?" I asked.

"We need a new consciousness, a new seriousness…a recognition that to live life fully, you have to be in life fully, away from the noise, away from the gadgets of modernity that take away your eyes and ears."

The man dug into his other jacket pocket, brought out another sheet of paper, and started to read from it:

"And I am the traveler, gathering stardust from a prairie moon, adding to the fickle music of our time an even tune, and building from the fluxions of dancing crystals little cocoons, home for the exiled linnet, hope for the drowning moon.

"Look! I promise you the world in a sheaf of grass! Look! Every glass of moon reflects the stars!"

In Search Of The Beauty And The Songs Of Birds

I've always had a fondness for birds.

My mother once walked a quarter of a mile chasing a mynah bird as it flew from tree to tree because I wanted to hear its entire song.

When visiting my grandmother in Madurai, India, I spent hours watching and following peacocks that roamed freely in the hillocks nearby.

In Madras, it was quite a thrill to watch a curtain of green move against a blue sky when hundreds of parrots took to the air.

Then there were the bulbuls filling the woodlands with music and their colorful presence.

In school, in Calcutta, I learned about the "light-winged Dryad of the trees."

I also encountered the thrush with his "full-hearted evensong/ Of joy illimited" who "Had chosen thus to fling his soul/ Upon the growing gloom" with "ecstatic sound."

"For brute beauty and valour and act," my English teacher, Mr. Biswas, asked us to turn the pages to Gerard Manley Hopkins' poem "The Windhover."

The sprung rhythm that Hopkins used was perfect for this poem: quick as the bird in graceful flight shifting to "the hurl and gliding" to rebuff the wind.

When I was living in Germany, the garden warblers would return to my garden in spring to build their nests.

How these tiny birds flying hundreds of miles knew how to find my dwelling in a crowded city is an amazing mystery. Perhaps they followed the stars. Perhaps their memories, sharper than mine, brought them back to a friendly place in the sun, like a compass brings a sailor home.

Whatever magic or science brought them there, I was always happy for their company.

At the Presidio in San Francisco, I found the entrance to the park lined with eucalyptus trees. Rows of these trees formed a stately archway, and the distinct aroma from the leaves sent forth an invitation. As soon as I wandered in, I noticed that the canopy was alive with the playful antics of parrots.

A mile away was the grand view of the Golden Gate Bridge, but rising steel and grand architecture had to wait for a curtain call from the choreography of green feathers.

In Rome, also, a colony of parrots in the palm trees that stood across from the Spagna Metro engaged my attention, as I made my way to the Spanish Steps.

I visited this iconic location on numerous occasions, and my wife, Maria, who is a bigger fan of birds than I am, always bid the parrots goodnight as we made our way back to the metro.

At Yosemite National Park, Maria fell in love with the calling of the yellow-rumped warbler.

Warblers are active birds, and they flit about in the branches of the trees with great alacrity. So, one literally has to chase their songs.

Living in El Paso, I was most grateful for the hummingbirds that visited the ocotillo blooms in spring and early summer. Their hover and dash, more eloquent and advanced than any form of modern transportation, seemed like something out of a futuristic novel.

I am equally grateful for the mockingbird, — so tiny, and yet so full of song!

Each morning, as I sit in my office composing a poem or balancing the checkbook, my work is interrupted by the lovely strains emanating from the treetop nearby.

If a wrong number should creep into the calculations, or a rhyme go awry, who am I to complain?

What better way to start the morning than with the sounds of a trickster who masquerades as an entire symphony.

Parks Offer An Oasis For The Soul, And So Much More

I have a great fondness for parks. Under open skies, and paths lined with majestic oaks or shade-giving elms, parks offer a cornucopia of delights.

I would go so far as to say that parks define the soul of a city. Show me a city where parks are plentiful and well-maintained, and I will show you a city where art and culture flourish, and children are happy.

This is not an extraordinary claim to make.

Take Forest Park in St. Louis, for example. This 1300-acre park is not just for long walks, boating, and fishing. One goes there to visit the zoo, attend an opera performance, or to spend a few hours at the art, science, or history museum.

A section of the park called Art Hill is also the setting in summer for Shakespeare's plays performed outdoors. What better way to enjoy "Romeo and Juliet" than out in the open with the stars overhead chiming their magic onto the dialog.

Another gem of a park I visited is the Golden Gate Park in San Francisco. With the Japanese Tea Garden, the Conservatory of Flowers, a redwood trail through the botanical garden, Stow Lake, and the M.H. de Young Memorial Museum, the park can occupy one's attention for an entire day, and then call for a return visit.

What makes these experiences special is the abundance of nature which offers relief from the city, crowds, and noise. Also, the aesthetics of these parks allow visitors to reflect, and to find inner peace.

At Balboa Park in San Diego, I met a German couple on vacation with their teenage daughter.

I did not see the daughter at first, because she was sitting on a bench at a distance working on some sketches.

"She is studying to be an artist," the dad explained. "She loves California. It truly inspires her."

A park may not be a rain forest or a Mount Kilimanjaro, but it points us to possibilities.

A trail in a park offers an invitation to an adventurous trail in some remote woods, and the well-planned, well-arranged beauty of parks teaches us to grab every golden hour between sunrise and sunset. Quickly we learn that we cannot allow our days to get lost in uncontemplated, spiritually supine existence.

Parks also manage to bring us to an understanding that nature, to quote Wolfgang von Goethe, "is the living, visible garment of God."

A park also offers other benefits that are self-constructed. One can fly a kite, throw a frisbee, or sit on a bench and read a book.

Of these activities, the last has always had a special appeal for me.

Sitting against the trunk of a tree in the Maidan in Calcutta, I would take out a book from my satchel and start reading it out loud.

This park stretched for miles starting at the Victoria Memorial, and I was free to be vocal and express myself without drawing any attention.

I could be dour as Sylvia Plath, or lilting and flamboyant as Dylan Thomas, for I had the audience of grass, trees, and sky all to myself.

And no list of delights a park offers can be complete without mentioning the picnic.

Just as a poem is changed by the surroundings in which it is read, the quality of food is enhanced by a picnic setting.

Open air clothes the foods in rich flavor, and sweetens the wine of conversation.

In fact, it is not stretching the truth to say that a park can be as painterly as a canvas, as majestic as a poem, and as sumptuous as a feast.

Nature Offers Perfect Getaway From Chaotic World

The city is too full of noise and discord. That's why I like getting away to the quiet parts of the country, like our national parks and nature refuges.

Off-season, you can be in the midst of the most wonderful aspects of nature and not hear a single human voice!

In May, my wife and I visited the J.N. "Ding" Darling National Wildlife Refuge in Sanibel Island in Florida.

If there was a protest somewhere in America where a mob burned the American flag and did battle with the police, we neither heard about it nor saw it.

Instead, our attention was focused on three anhinga fledglings that, on unsteady feet and untested wings, were trying to leave the confines of their nest. Below them, an alligator waited patiently for a misstep to occur.

If somewhere in America a politician was making old promises in a new vein, the words did not carry through to us.

Somehow, the future rested on the next step one of the anhinga babies would take.

In the refuge, we also went in search of the roseate spoonbill. The spoonbill numbers are on the decline, and so the paucity of sightings was not surprising. It was on our third visit to the park that we finally made our first sighting of the spoonbill. What a thrill to come across the sudden pink in the green waters of a pond!

If a flood of bad news came over the television set, it did not disturb the prelapsarian Eden where fish swam under a canopy of lily pads.

In the Shark Valley at the Everglades National Park, a soft-shell turtle came out to greet us. Maria heard warblers in the treetops.

On the Loop Road, not far away, in the Monet-like canvases of water, alligators made twin islands of head-and-eyes and scaly-backs.

The diurnal chaos of the world seemed far away.

At low tide, when new stretches of sand were exposed at the beaches of Sanibel Island and Captiva, we loved to go hunting for shells. There were so many to pick from, and of such great variety. My favorites were the fan-shaped cockle, the banded tulip, the lightning whelk, and conch.

The houses of some of the conch were occupied, so I set them back in the water gently. It is best to let tides write the pages of their book.

If the world was being made to stand on its head by activists of diverse ilk, I couldn't have cared less.

The strong elegance and powerful beauty of an osprey sitting on a branch near Lighthouse Beach in Sanibel was sufficient proof that, away from the mad cataract of human speech and actions, the world rested in equilibrium and uprightness.

The scurrying sandpipers looking for food played tag with the waves. The ibis' walk in the water was an exquisite ballet.

At sunset, the pelicans flew overhead in striking formation signaling the gold, red, and orange of the sky to settle into sleep.

If the world was in turmoil with the foolishness of man, there was no sign of it anywhere.

It was the crepuscular hour. Waves lapped the shore. Later, as the blanket of quietude and solitude was spread across the sands, moonbeams caressed the branches of the tree where the osprey had been perched.

I thought about the anhinga babies, on the cusp of independence, resting for the night.

Everywhere was a prayer.

The quiet song of the earth, in which man is but minuscule, played on like a lullaby.

"The harp at nature's advent strung," as Whittier wrote, continued to play.

Walk In The Middle of God's Creations, And Rejoice

The Rose with sleep still wet in her eyes, and promised with a future as bright as a prince's stride, looks to the sky where dark clouds are beginning to gather.

Was it thunder she heard? Will the weather turn virulent? And what of all the possibilities that were petal-soft and dew-fresh? Will they come to fruition?

Let the past be past; and if a sunbeam was not gathered at heaven's height, let it be so, without regret.

Wipe the sleep from your eyes, and reach upward from the earth where a small tune calls out to drums and fife.

Nothing is secure as silk. All moments pass: even peach- and plum-hour.

The moth is on the wood, and the rust is on the treasure.

Therefore, twirl with birdsong and move on horse-wings to a comelier sight.

Be heroic. The world may revolve away from near delights, and the glass may reveal some cardinal truth or magic flute to have a flaw, but let the charm and reach of spring keep a firm, assured hold on things.

Let the 'now' carry its flag in the sweet air of the thrush, and a trove of petals define delight.

Speak of greatness: the rounded spheres of Ptolemy's music; the universe of lilt and magic. Speak of the curve that brings rapture to stone and spire.

Laetare! All that is mangled and melded have the single flame of God in them. Every inch of the path that is twisted, and every hour of the tired, worn shoes, have in their frames hosannas from high.

Cast aside doubt and trepidation.

Behold how from a pool of loss and sadness, the rose climbs to redemption's perch.

Speak of love: how amorous silk runs its course towards secret, scented woods; how a kingdom is won by a sprig of lilac and proud poesy.

"The winter is past, the rain is over and gone." God is love.

Do you hear an extraordinary music sometimes in the simplest things, at the quietest hour? Have you stood in boundless moonlight and wondered where you are headed? And then, did you hear the bent branch forever singing to the river?

Watch how the coin of love admits everything into forever.

Think not of temporal and fleeting things. Where oceans collide, there too the light is evanescent. And the songs in a thousand sails that move the boat toward adventure and profit are sparse compared to the song in a prayer of grass.

Let rosebud come to the rescue, defying gravity, to get an old picture back.

Let a flutter of leaves and a subtle breeze at the shoulder yield once more lovers caught in the spray of the cataract's play.

And then watch how the prodigious arm bends to gather up the child.

Nothing is ever lost, for divinity's path stretches well beyond the stars.

Even where the stars repose in silent tapestry, there is between one twinkle and the next the full measure of their speech and songs, as though the silence were but the sweet cloth that ties one note to the next.

Unscratched, the word moves in the branches, carrying a friendly song to the far banks of the river — the melody is soft like childhood and, yet, touched by the gift of age, precise; and I am encouraged to look at life from an ageless rise.

The cadenzas will keep.

The sweep of time sweetens the ride.

Riches And Gold When Our Kingdom Is In The Open Fields

People own jewels, and many wear them, even if they do not hold them up to the light to see heaven in their scintillations.

Possessions are wonderful things when their core comes into being as they take us beyond ownership to a place without compass or coordinates — to a country called Joy..

As children, our kingdom was in the open fields. No one among us owned them, and yet they were ours.

When we were "famous among the barns" and carefree, we were peculiarly aware of the butterfly in the grass and the songs in the brook.

The eye was full and the ear in tune with the sounds of the universe; and the rainbow in the spray of water fascinated us.

We grew up and lost the kingdom, as the crown of clouds dissolved in the air of purpose and direction.

What we hold in our hands will slip away from our grips soon enough, but what we hold with our eyes and hearts and celebrate will enjoy a longevity that can be as long as life, or even the ages.

In "Middlemarch," Rosamond Vincy cannot contemplate life withouts plates and cutlery. For her, life has meaning and purpose inside the hustle-bustle and noise of society.

However, when the house falls silent and we have ourselves for company, ostentation and the transient mirth of strangers cannot bring us comfort or satisfaction.

Then are we forced to look at the accoutrements of our soul, and at things that hold beauty in them, rather than carry them from window to window.

Also in "Middlemarch," we find Edward Casaubon, a scholarly gentleman on a mission to unlock the key to all mythologies.

Though he wanders dim-lit, windowless corridors of knowledge in the fulness of his erudition, he has lost touch with simple joys in this world. Better scholar is he who knows how to swing from tree branches than the man who is burdened with the weight of books and has no spring in his steps.

Things that we profess to own can desert us either through loss or loss of usefulness. Thieves can break through and steal what we own, or else they can become corrupted by moth and rust (Matthew 6:19)

Possessions are for young people who see the world as endless and belonging to them entirely. As we grow older, we must divest ourselves of things that are superfluous and merely occupy space.

I have nothing against possessions that bring joy. My prejudice is only against possessions that are guarded, that are tucked away, or serve as mere status symbols.

Silas Marner found out that "gold that was hidden away from daylight, was deaf to the song of birds, and started to no human tones" was not capable of bringing joy.

I have a friend who owns an estate. He has a lot of wooded area behind his house and a sumptuous garden.

My friend said to me once, "I think you come here mostly to talk to my gardener."

I denied it, of course, but I must confess that my conversations with the gardener are illuminating and fun-filled. My friend, on the other hand, takes little interest in the things that fall outside the material world.

To be honest, I'd readily forgo a social gathering at the home of Jay Gatsby for some innocuous chat about the Columbian monkshood or the curve-billed thrasher.

Silas found more gold in the locks of little Eppie's hair than in all the coins he ever earned.

A Day Without Digital Brings Rich Rewards

It is amazing how much can be accomplished by disengaging from digital activities for even one day. Until you try it, it is difficult to gain an appreciation for how much time gets freed up when you are not sitting in front of the screen.

Visit any site on the Internet, and the sidebar comes up replete with suggestions for new things to explore.

Knowing all your wonts and predilections, the ubiquitous, all-seeing Eye offers recommendations for where to shop, where to eat, what movies to see, and what other sites to visit, — to name just a few.

One drink leads to another, and before long you get blotto on the Internet.

With these thoughts swirling in my mind, I decided not to switch on any digital device for one entire day of a weekend.

Sitting in the office in front of an empty computer screen, I thought I had best arrange all the clutter that was sitting atop the table.

Many items that needed discarding had been allowed to stay on because the time needed to inspect these items for their usefulness had been usurped by the Eye on the Internet.

After the tabletop regained its respectability, I decided to write a letter - a real letter — which I had been putting off for some time.

It is so much easier to dictate a few lines — mistakes and all — into the cellphone, but an old-fashioned letter takes time. Thoughts have to be formulated for content, grammar, syntax and style before they are entered on paper.

The world is a different place when you are standing on real ground and key strokes cannot create a mountain or a trench.

Away from the rows of keys that offered digital travel with alacrity, I found myself with so much time on my hands that I could have sat under a tree and whistled a tune or read from a book of essays.

I did neither, but sat on a chair in the backyard and watched the birds. I saw something I had not seen before. One grackle took a piece of bread that my wife Maria had thrown on the grass, took it to the birdbath, and dipped it in the water before eating it.

I guess he liked the bread soft, or was he fastidious about his food being clean?

Later in the morning, I took time to bend a few limbs of the lemon tree with weights, for they had developed an unwarranted ambition to reach for the sky.

The digital world is all about speed and the quick availability of things, whereas nature and things of beauty demand leisure and contemplation.

Whether we brush past the lilies or gather them in our hands depends on our attitude and disposition: are we going somewhere in a hurry or blindly, or have we allowed ourselves the luxury of looking around, especially in quiet and uncommon places?

Much of Saturday's afternoon and evening lay before me as an unpainted canvas, and I could mix the colors any way I wanted to paint a picture.

Of all the pictures I painted that day, one stands out in my mind, and it involved the moon.

Without the interference of digital devices, my mind felt strangely free, and it is with this freedom that I embraced the moon, nearly full, "with its world of poetry and oracular suggestions" — to quote Thoreau.

"In such a night let me abroad remain / Till morning breaks, and all's confused again," wrote the poet.

By turning off digital devices we are taking away some of the confusion that belongs to the day, and replacing them with a panoply of perspectives that looks kindly on beauty and grace.

A Conversation With Grass

"Nothing so cleanses the dross out of a man
as the creation of beauty,
or the pursuit of truth." — Will Durant

I woke to the morning with a whisper from a blade of grass. "The wind that brushes against my back," said Grass, "has come from afar and bids you pay attention to the landscape."

"What landscape?" I asked, rubbing the sleep out of my eyes.

"From East to West, from North to South, the sky is yours. What pictures will you paint on that canvas today? The land beckons you in all directions. What destinations will you seek?"

It was not my wont to contemplate such hefty topics early in the morning. Grass must have read my mind, for it said, "Lest you think the matter has no great urgency, allow me to show you how quietly but steadily the hours run out of the glass, transforming prodigiousness to want, abilities to handicaps, and the concrete to abstractions."

"Look at the drop of dew that is my crown," continued Grass. "Peer inside. While you were away, something quietly touched green leaf to yellow. Flying flutes moved to your country. A tune tumbled out. And then, a soft breeze picked it up and carried it into memory. Through the leaves, across the fields, did you hear the soft coin of a melody?"

"I think I understand your message," I said. "Philosophers and poets have written about the evanescence of all moments; how the moment not grasped may become a moment lost forever."

"And so unto the light," said Grass. "Let bugle sound your full fine thoughts against receding shadows. Let the flower of reason and joy be upon every easting road."

"But is it enough just to be in beauty, to celebrate its abundance?" I asked.

Our conversation was interrupted. A butterfly burst upon the scene to hold a causerie with Grass. In the distance, a hummingbird trained its beak into the hollow of a flower.

"Our job, and it is a most important one," said Grass, "is to carry beauty's pollen to other places. It is by this journey that beauty is wedded to truth, and truth moves into the country of justice."

A line from Will Durant flashed in my mind. He had written, "Nothing so cleanses the dross out of a man as the creation of beauty, or the pursuit of truth."

I saw Jackson Pollock perched on a ladder, dripping paint onto a large canvas.

I saw the music of a symphony bounce gently from the dome of a cathedral, travel to the large columns, and fall like powder or motes of sunlight, bringing serenity and sanctity to the milieu.

Lotuses bloomed in a pond. A village dirt road that ran alongside the pond soon turned busy as a large group of marchers filled its length as far as the eye could see. At the head of the group, I saw Mahatma Gandhi, walking stick in hand, marching to the sea to make salt. The act had the beauty and strength of the lotus.

Grass said: "Be full in Beauty, Truth, and Justice. Obey the flame of each dawn; ride the sun's chariot towards life's vibrant displays; and find heaven in a polyphony of happy sounds."

I looked up. The sky was full of color and the air stitched with felicitous songs.

Adieu, Gypsy … He Was a Grand Adventurer And A Connoisseur Of Life

He could have been a Magellan or a Vasco de Gama. His heart was fearless, and he loved travel and adventure. In every country he visited, his admirers were legion, for his charms were eloquent and his joie de vivre infectious.

As can be expected of one who was peripatetic and carried his importance on his sleeve, he was a connoisseur of food. And because he indulged in haute cuisine, sometimes to excess, his physical appearance was more round than linear.

In casual repose, he resembled still life, but he could put on a burst of speed when needed, and stare down enemies ten times his size.

A bundle of contradictions, he could be meek as a mouse or threatening as a tiger.

He loved nature and was partial to the multi-layered symphony of a hummingbird that called out from the apex of the pine tree that fronted his house. The staccato rhythms of the woodpecker fascinated him.

Curious as a baby, he studied all moving things, and many things that did not move. In short, he was a natural scientist.

No one, least of all my wife Maria and I, put an age on him. He seemed ageless.

It is a sad truth of life that its river has bends and, by and by, one gets to a place where the water moves but slowly, and its song begins to fade. The great traveler who had leapt across walls, shot across streets, and marched boldly into unknown territories, was suddenly stricken with arthritis in his knee.

In just a few days, the perennial adventurer, the swashbuckling hero, was reduced to an attenuated figure who had to drag his stricken leg to go from place to place.

Worse still, the doctor declared that his kidneys were failing, and his body was shutting down. There was nothing to do; it was just old age asserting itself.

The malfunctioning kidneys were producing toxins, and he turned away from the best cooking Maria offered him. Pain, too, had entered the picture, scratching the night with its odious sound.

"I'm afraid I don't have good news for you," said the doctor, studying the X-rays and pointing to various aspects of a blood test. "He should be put to sleep. He's a tough boy, but he can't last more than a few days, and he will suffer a great deal of pain in the interim."

And so the decision was made to bid Gypsy farewell.

Before the doctor administered the final medication to end his suffering, Maria talked to Gypsy and told him that she loved him. She made a clicking sound with her fingernails, a codeword that Gypsy understood. We both petted him.

Through the mist of sedation, Gypsy must have heard our comforting voices and felt our touch. Then it was over. The body was free of pain … only the shell remained.

Maria and I petted the body that had once carried the soul that had given us so much delight. We cried for the loss of so dear a one, but were happy, too, that he had gone past the gates of pain.

Maria had daily conversations with Gypsy, and they shared a special bond. She will miss him the most.

He, too, will miss her, for no angel was more angel than Maria was to him.

We Hear The Voice Of God All Around Us

Near the Watchtower in the Grand Canyon, where one can enjoy a stunning panorama, are posted these lines from Psalm 66: "All the earth worships Thee; they sing praises to Thee, sing praises to Thy name."

These are fitting words, for when one is in the presence of the awe-inspiring beauty of nature, one's thoughts automatically turn to God.

I saw God in the foothills of the Himalayas when morning broke its egg on the slopes of the mountains. And as the day spun its story forward, He was there in the smallest of sounds and in the highest of heights.

Among the things that are marked by age that flicker and fade, the strength of God makes in one hour a kingdom that is resplendent forever. The colors are rich and the sky is warm when we are in the embrace of Grace.

I saw God again in the playful steps of a stream leading toward the hour when all the continents became as one. The pebble rounded to infinite smoothness announced gently that all of geography is God.

Have you noticed that when evening's sunlight lays her carpet on alfalfa fields, or when the sulfurs race across wind-bent fields, the air assumes an extraordinary quality that carries intimations of divinity? At the Grand Canyon, the subtle copper-green of rocks was in a marriage with gardens of russet and gold. The blue ribbon of the Colorado snaked its way through the depths.

The mighty Colorado is replete with the voices of men and their accomplishments, but truth be told the glory of it all belongs to God. There is a song that starts in the grass and finishes at the crown of giant trees. The moth carries it as much as the condor. The flame of it offers respite and succor.

There is a song that is short as the walk of a caterpillar and long as the Colorado is long. A child and a man are both privy to it, for the language of God is mighty but simple.

Near the Watchtower in the Grand Canyon, I sat on a bench and, in solitude, surveyed the landscape before me.

At the base of the canyon I imagined mighty activity and the roar of the waters, but in front of me was eerie stillness which the broom of the wind swept away from time to time.

Man toils as the river does to cut the rocks in front of it, but the chisel and the chiseled belong to God. If the architecture makes the heart leap, it is because we recognize in it the hand of God.

And whosoever hears the music that is in the soil and the stone shall raise a cathedral or a kingdom, for the great works of man are inspired by the great Hand that guides the heart and the mind to glory.

The hammer of the river and the hammer of the artist are one and the same.

The curtain of the Grand Canyon is a cascade of colors. Every color there is poured out of an infinite drum to make coats brindled, mottled, and bedecked.

From the quiet spot where I sat, I heard the church bells from lands near and far, and a voice saying: "Let the heavens rejoice, let the earth be glad; let the sea resound, and all that is in it. Let the field be jubilant, and everything in them; let all the trees of the forest sing for joy."

Summer Unleashes Surprises

Summer brings on many surprises. From the early blooming of the purple leaf plum to the arrival of the hummingbirds among cactus flowers, there is feast for the eyes and music for the ears in every sweep of the hour.

I no longer set the alarm on the clock. Long before it is my wont to wake up, a mockingbird alerts me to the day with acoustical acrobatics.

As the sun's rays touch the tips of an army of cypresses, then bend down to caress the pink filaments of the mimosa, and dance their way down and come to rest on a green carpet of grass, I think about the many ways by which nature brings meaning and richness to our lives.

Henry David Thoreau understood the prodigious gifts of nature best when he said, "I have traveled a great deal in Concord."

The pyramids are a sight to behold, and who can forget a trek in the foothills of the Himalayas, or a boat ride on the Danube, but there is pure magic in watching a dove build its nest in the branches of a palmetto.

In the mornings, I peer into the green of the palm, and catch sight of a fraction of the nest. It is well hidden. I would not have found it if it had not been for my wife Maria who keeps careful accounting of nature's goings-on.

Day after day, I see the mother dove patiently sitting on her nest, waiting for new life to push its way through the shell's barrier.

I think of Saint Francis' long work "Canto del amore" which speaks of love for all of God's creation — and inspires in us the notion that love is a powerful life-altering force.

I am also reminded of these lines from "Saint Francis and the Sow," a poem by Galway Kinnell: "The bud/ stands for all things/ even for those things that don't flower,/ for everything flowers, from within, of self-blessing …"

So, welcome to the pyramid of the rose, the Danube of the wisteria, the towering peak of the ocotillo.

Welcome, also, to the Taj Mahal of the peacock, the royal barge of the grackle, and the temple of the caparisoned elephant.

As Kinnell pointed out in his poem, a deeper knowledge of any living thing brings us face to face with beauty.

At the crepuscular hour, Maria came running to me once with great excitement and announced that a low-flying owl had startled her out of her reverie in the backyard.

A full moon smiled upon this incident.

Said the moon: "An owl is an ordinary creature until you look at it extraordinarily."

So are a blade of grass, a raindrop on a broad lotus leaf, and a scent of jasmine made special to embrace the circumference of the earth.

"Earth's crammed with heaven," wrote Elizabeth Barrett Browning, "and every common bush afire with God."

When I was a public-school teacher, I would take my students to the park once in a while for writing exercises. Looking is a quotidian activity, but seeing is another matter altogether. A tree is more than a tree; and a cloud can be an ocean.

All roads are golden, for the gold is in our eyes.

The World Is A Magical Place

A robin that was hop-hop-hopping along on a cold November morning espied me looking at a pink rose that had opened in full defiance of the weather, and said, "A lovely day to be singing and dancing, is it not?"

"I am thankful for the day, and your ebullience; and for all the stories you carry on your little wings," I answered.

"It is the little things in life that matter, after all," the robin continued. "Look at this Mexican elderberry. Its roots are old and weak, but still it rejoices in every butterfly that flits by, and every cloud that passes overhead. Even in infirmity, it gathers all its strength to put forth clusters of white blossoms for our enjoyment."

"I, too, am thankful for all the little things. Why, just moments ago, I saw you with your partner performing a ballet in the air. Your flight was perfectly harmonized, as if you knew exactly what was in your partner's thoughts. That's a little miracle, is it not?"

"Everything is a miracle," the robin answered.

"How true," I said. "A peacock's feather, a mynah's song, and a rainbow in the sky — they all stirred strong emotions in my heart when I was only so tall. I knew then that the world had height, and I wanted to touch every aspect of it that was covered in new light."

I remembered Cato's soliloquy on the immortality of the soul: "If there is a Power above us, — and that there is, all Nature cries aloud through all her works — He must delight in virtue; and that which He delights in must be happy."

Across the street, two children came out of their home with springs in their steps, and started playing hopscotch on the sidewalk. The squares on the ground were drawn with flamboyant chalk, and the diagram was a winged bird as tall as the sky.

"I am thankful for children, too," I said, "for they have pure eyes and pure minds."

"The tragedy of growing up," the robin posited, "is that we lose the child in us. Real maturity happens when we rediscover that lost child. It is only for the second child that the sky opens out its charms."

"Yes indeed," I said. "Through recovered innocence alone we see the world anew in all its rightful glory."

An army of white, billowy clouds marched across the sky, waving the flag of man's accomplishments, from the fire in the cave to the fire across the universe.

"I go from here to there chasing seasons, and I do not know quite how it happens. Much has been accomplished, and much yet needs to be done," said the robin.

I thought about the perfect ellipse of the earth's orbit that makes all life possible. I thought about the peculiar dance of water's density near freezing that keeps the lower strata of ponds and lakes safe for marine life. I thought about the magnet in the hummingbird's brain that brings it to my yard every spring. I thought about the wonders that remain wonders long after science has connected the spheres and made a bridge of understanding.

"I am thankful for the mind," I said to the robin, "for it gives us this moment, and all other moments. We may arrive at each day adding and subtracting, carrying joy in one hand and some grief in the other for things that have passed us by, but the world is a magical place, and life is precious."

"I have my colors and my songs, and I hope I have given pleasure with both, perhaps to touch the speech of angels," the robin said. With that, he sang a cheerful song, and bid me adieu.

Make Poetry A "Feast of April" In Our Classrooms

In El Paso, February fools nature into thinking that spring has arrived, so that by the time April rolls around, the birds, the flowers, and the butterflies are in the full stretch of their spring dance.

This is the time for poetry — for reading it, and writing it — and a teacher must use stratagems and his persuasive powers to draw students into the web of poetry, just as surely as April draws the hummingbirds to nectar.

Many people suffer from the notion that poetry is less substantive than prose, and more difficult to grasp, but nothing could be further from the truth.

It is true that poetry is not stretched out like prose in a continuum where all the connections are made clear.

We enjoy a story knowing full well it is not our story: The characters move and think with the orchestrations of the author.

In sharp contrast, a poem has gaps and silences — ellipses, to quote Joyce Carol Oates — that must be filled in by the reader to complete the poem's meaning.

This is because in poetry the language opens out to the reader, whereas in a short story or a novel the language closes in on the characters.

"What did the poet mean?" asks a student in my class.

"This is where you come in," I reply. "The poet is not there to tell us, and so you must provide the answer yourself. In this way you become a part of the poem."

By all rights, poetry should gain manyfold in popularity, for it is a highly democratic instrument of thought, pitching a capacious tent for its understanding.

It is also replete with freedoms, for we are not trapped by facts and reason; and half-knowledge will suffice — what Keats called "negative capability."

My students in sixth grade loved poetry.

Once they understood the use of metaphors in verse, they couldn't have enough of them. Gone was clumsy and baggy speech. In came the flutes and the violins.

Of course, poetry demands precision of language suitable for prosody, but, where genius does not supply it, the skill may be acquired with time and practice.

I gave students a list of poems to memorize, if they wanted to engage in the process — for I figured that such freedom would draw more to the task than a teacher's command.

I was not disappointed.

Many gave excellent recitations of Frost's "The Road Not Taken," Shakespeare's "Sonnet 116" and Whitman's "O Captain! My Captain!"

One boy — just to show off — even committed Frost's "Mending Wall" to memory, and poured forth the words in front of his classmates with great elan and ostentation.

The difficulty with poetry exists until the difficulty goes away with the recognition that it is both a vibrant and a friendly medium.

Poetry is also vastly engaging, because, where successful, it provides linguistic prompts that draw the reader into the picture, into the argument, or into the contemplation of events and thoughts.

Consider these lines:

"When I remember much / the weather in the city changes; / Because the wind remembers her name, / our conversation is exact and long."

How wide is the berth here for speculation? How numerous are the invitations for engagement?

In trying to understand what the poet was thinking, we begin to understand ourselves. A treasure trove of our own memories opens up, and we understand the weather in "our own city."

In our classrooms, let us make poetry a "Feast of April."

And let the fare include all varieties of ordinary and exotic items fit for the palate of a king.

A Tree, A Sparrow, And The Circle Of Life Observed Closely

In the front yard of my house sits a Mexican elderberry tree that, for the past few years, has been trying assiduously to put forth leaves and blossoms.

For all its efforts, though, the verdure seems to belong to an earlier time, and the gnarled trunk and branches have a grim and austere countenance that spells age in unequivocal terms.

Looking at the tree in late spring, I allowed my mind to become colored by a melancholy that is the natural destination of contemplation when it is focused on the passage of time, and it seemed to me that Old Man Tree was looking at the world wisely, and somewhat defiantly — an image that brought to mind Santiago putting out to sea and going after the big fish for one last time.

"Do not go gentle into that good night. Rage, rage against the dying of the light," poet Dylan Thomas wrote to his father "there on the sad height," and the elderberry seemed to be doing just that.

Two weeks ago, my wife, Maria, noticed that a hole that opened from the underside of one of the branches was, in fact, a nest. She came to this conclusion after she espied a small, yellow beak at the mouth of the hole.

The yellow rhombus on a gray canvas of space could have been an element in a Miro painting or a Calder construction. The art appeared in response to a sparrow that had alighted on a limb that grew from the base of the hole.

A great cacophony ensued, and it was quieted only after the sparrow deposited some food into the gaping mouth.

The Old Man, I thought to myself, was still sanguine because his weak arm supported a stage replete with extraordinary drama. The feeding ritual was incessant as the mama and the papa sparrows took turns bringing food to the fledgling.

Nature is prodigiously layered with miracles; no sooner had the curtain fallen on one than it was raised on another.

Three days after the discovery of the nest, Maria and I were going for our morning constitutional when our steps were arrested on the porch by the sight of a baby sparrow. It was a bundle of curiosity, and made no attempt to hop or fly away.

On the same day, in the evening, we saw it on the front lawn being fed by one of its parents. Each time the parent approached the baby, its wings shivered with excitement, and its mouth opened into the air to receive food.

When the parent strategically flew away and sought a temporary perch in the neighbor's pine tree, the youngster crossed the lawn and the road with insouciant steps. Along the way, it flapped its wings desultorily, but failed to gain altitude.

Failure, however, was short-lived.

Next morning, when Maria was watering the lawn, she noticed a familiar figure perched on the lowest branch of the elderberry. Maria tried to approach it, but the once-congenial fellow, now with caution on his side, took to the air with alacrity.

The world had changed forever.

A tree has many stories to tell, and many lessons to teach us, if we should care to listen to its daily discourses.

Stubby Gets By With A Little Help From Friends

During the winter months, my wife, Maria, feeds the birds that live near our home. In the great equation of nature, Maria might be a gratuitous player, but ask the birds, and they will tell you a different story.

In early March, when the El Paso sun starts to trick the purple plum trees into bloom, Maria starts thinning the amount of seeds and food crumbs she sprinkles onto the backyard lawn.

This attenuation of hospitality that the pigeons, the mourning doves, the Inca doves, and the sparrows might feel is easily mitigated by the food plate that nature opens up to April skies. This year, though, the story's script had to be rewritten, because Stubby came into the picture.

During the usual afternoon feeding session, Maria noticed that one mourning dove was exercising a great deal of industry to pick up some seeds: the bobbing motion of his head was noticeably pronounced, and he displayed an intensity that verged on anxiety. Closer inspection revealed that the dove had a deformed beak. "Look at his beak," cried Maria. "It's not pointy; it's flat. No wonder he's having such a difficult time picking up his food. I'll call him, Stubby … poor thing."

The birds on the grass were like chess pieces constantly seeking positions of advantage to get at the food. Stubby, though, stayed put, and tried to get all that he could within a small circumference.

"I can't stop feeding them even though spring is almost here," Maria said. "What will become of Stubby?"

Right then the decision was made to purchase more bags of seed and to extend the feeding season.

After Stubby came into the picture, Maria started paying more attention to him at feeding time, and she noticed that even with her help, Stubby still used his smarts to leverage the amount of food he could gather.

While the other birds sat on the wall and waited patiently for Maria to distribute the seeds, Stubby flew down from his perch and landed not more than a yard away from Maria's feet.

For a brief time, the bird-to-benefactor ratio was 1:1.

This gave Stubby enough time to pack away a small part of his dinner before the field became agitated with the hither-and-thither peregrinations of mostly grey wings.

Stubby knew that in order to get his full share of the food, he had to let down his guard somewhat. He took a chance with Maria, and it worked.

I wonder if the other birds thought of him as heroic or impetuous … a Patton taking a calculated risk toward a spectacular victory, or a callow soldier making a terrible blunder.

It didn't matter what they thought of him, though, for Maria had concluded that he was a brainy bird with character and charisma.

Then one day, a surprising event occurred. All the birds had returned to their various homes in advance of the crepuscular light, when Maria noticed that Stubby was sitting on a shelf just outside the kitchen window.

He had come for a second helping, and Maria obliged.

Now Stubby visits us also in the evening. When he arrives with the flock, he might be a member of the retinue in a royal procession, but in the evening when he leaves, he is clearly king.

Catch The Song In A River, Chase A Mynah Bird

French artist Claude Monet wanted to capture the optics and special flavor of a scene in each of his "series" paintings.

To that end, he painted each scene, whether it was the facade of Rouen Cathedral, or a grain stack, innumerable times — at different times of the day, and during different months.

His purpose was to mix the poetry of time with the chemistry of paint.

Monet undertook this journey because he was in awe of all that he beheld, and he wanted to celebrate beauty.

Recently, I watched a song-and-dance routine from an old Hindi film "Talash."

In "Aaj to junali raat ma," Sharmila Tagore gives a bravura performance — so completely does she abandon herself to the joy of dancing, so completely is she in technical control, and so sanguine are her emotional perceptions, that her performance leaps toward transcendence.

I had first heard the song nearly four decades ago (I never saw the movie), and now I was thrilled not only to rediscover the romantic lyrics, which came flooding back, but to find new poetry in the dance's energetic and compelling choreography.

Speaking of poetry, Nobel Laureate Seamus Heaney wrote: "I want to profess the surprise of poetry as well as its reliability; I want to celebrate its given, unforeseeable thereness, the way it enters our field of vision and animates our physical and intelligent being."

I have frequently been taken "there," to a different place, to encounter and assimilate the surprises offered by song, dance, painting and poetry. However, the "here" that prepared me for those peregrinations was the gift of upbringing and education.

My great-grandmother Pattitha taught me the songs that lived in the Alwaye river.

My mother indulged me by chasing a mynah bird so that I could hear its full song.

My father told me stories of the constellations as we lay on charpais and looked at the night sky over New Delhi.

And my uncle, Periappa, mottled his conversations so felicitously with Shakespearean quotes, that it was impossible to avoid delving into the two volumes of the bard's plays that occupied a special place in the living room's bookcase.

"The fireflies, twinkling among leaves, make the stars wonder," wrote poet Rabindranath Tagore.

Looking down, or looking up, there were wonders, and as a young lad, and then as a young man, I was acutely aware of the surfeit and of man's tiny grasp.

At school, my teachers filled my head with thoughts that "like sparks rode on winged surprises."

In one classroom, there was the poetry of Kabir Das, Tulsi Das, and Meera Bhai; in another, the poetry of Percy Bysshe Shelley, Gerard Manley Hopkins, and Thomas Gray.

By the end of middle school, I had memorized many great poems.

The accomplishment I cherished the most was my memorization of "Elegy Written In A Country Churchyard."

In mathematics, proofs in geometry were executed with such panache that when the teacher shouted "QED," I felt like clapping. It was as though Pavarotti had hit a high C in Donizetti's "La Fille du Regiment."

If we can get our children to appreciate the joy and beauty in life, educating them would become an easier task.

Take A Look At Nature's Wonders, And You'll Be Amazed

"The artist," Winston Churchill wrote, "cannot be bored or left at a loose end. How much there is to admire and how little time there is to see it in!"

He wrote those words after he had decided to commit some of his energies to the brush that "hung poised, heavy with destiny, irresolute in the air."

It is not just the artist who must envy Methuselah, but the writer as well, for time is of the essence when the need exists to study the landscape, be it human or geographical, in great detail.

No great work of art or literature ever emerged from the journey of a mind as it moved briskly from leaf to leaf, or mountain to mountain, or country to country. It is when a seemingly commonplace event or sentiment is enshrined by a long, dedicated and loving look that its innate, God-centered greatness comes to fruition.

A life fully lived is also a work of art, and demands from the traveler the same solicitude.

Helen Keller once asked a friend who had just returned from a long walk in the woods what she had observed. "Nothing in particular," the friend had replied, casually, which struck Keller as being an extraordinarily empty statement.

Ironically, Keller had the advantage of her blindness to become submerged in the gamut of beauty surrounding her. For her friend -- vis-a-vis the walk in the woods -- the world existed merely as a backdrop to her corporeal actions.

Even though I was brought up on the poetry of Wordsworth and Shelley, and had been exposed at an early age to the ruminations of Thoreau at Walden, I was just as blind as Keller's friend, failing to read extraordinary stories in "the smooth skin of a silver birch, or the rough shaggy bark of a pine."

The challenge I have set for myself is to pay greater heed to the glories that surround me.

I must admit, however, that my efforts are frequently stymied by obduracy of habit.

Rather than give devout attention to the cathedral of a cumulus cloud, on numerous occasions, I have allowed some seemingly urgent, prosaic matter to obviate the enjoyment of such a delectation. And too often has the mockingbird's symphony been spurned on account of some mundane activity that could easily have been put aside.

In the early mornings, moisture-laden leaves appear greener, and the mountains have a purplish, romantic hue that the sun steals from them later in the day to render it a common brown.

Perhaps, because the air is thicker, even bird calls sound more mellifluous. All these, the eyes must see and the ears hear, but the mind, moving ahead like a scout, must ready the stage for these visitations.

Quite often, the magic is "in the moment," and unless the mind is ever at the ready to make capital from it, a life may become a collection of mostly "nothing-in-particular" experiences. Such penury will have been the result of attitude, not lack of opportunity.

If I am to inspire myself so that my eyes dance upward to embrace the April-delight of wisterias in bloom, then I must become baptized in the sights, sounds, smells and tactility of every aspect of this glorious existence.

Can A Word Be A Bird?

Gopal sat in the shade of a banyan tree and looked to the sky for inspiration. His teacher, Mr. Biswas, had asked his students to write a composition of not more than one paragraph in length describing an enchantment.

The sky, however, seemed stubbornly poised against giving suggestions; and even the wind refused to play among the leaves of the banyan tree.

"If only I had a starting sentence," thought Gopal, looking at the sheet of paper on his lap, which was replete with crossed-out lines, "then I could make some progress."

Just at that moment, Gopal heard the friendly clanging of a bicycle bell. Looking up, he saw Doraiswamy, who owned the only printing press in the village and published a newspaper, sporadically in tune with local happenings.

He was erudite and well-respected.

"School work?" asked the elder, alighting from his bicycle.

"Yes," said Gopal, and he proceeded to explain the nature of the assignment.

"No doubt, you are trying to think of a situation or a story that embraces the idea of enchantment. Instead, try to think of a subject, or an object, and then build enchantment around it ... with words."

"How do you do that?" asked Gopal.

"Take the word 'word', " said Doraiswamy. "Shall we say it's a boat, nimble as a dancer? It can sway forward or backward, bounce upward or downward, and curl sideways, in cushions of air that touch a village or a city. Release it in a river of moonbeam, and watch the stars dance."

"Can a word be a bird?" asked Gopal, excitement beginning to show on his face.

"Of course," said Doraiswamy. "The bird is in the curves and flourishes of your handwriting, or in your hair which is full of wild romance. It's full of new beginnings."

"A word is precise as a question," continued the interlocutor, "and wide as its response. It takes sunshine for a walk into unfamiliar and unknown places."

"I think I will choose this banyan tree for my composition," declared Gopal.

"Vat Vriksha: a worthy subject; full of possibilities and transcendence. Gautama sat under the banyan tree, meditated, and received enlightenment."

"But I still need a starting sentence," said Gopal.

"Close your eyes," said Doraiswamy. "Now tell me what you see."

"Trunks ... branches ... roots ... the sky."

"Yes ... yes ..," urged Doraiswamy.

"Now look at the tree as a butterfly looks at it from its gambols, or be the light that clothes it in the morning when the sun breaks its egg on the hillside. Fling your soul forward; go from leaf to leaf, country to country, sun to sun."

His teacher had told him to make the writing extraordinary: various, decorative, and unique.

Gopal reflected a while, and said to Doraiswamy, "In the canopy of bark and branches are bridges, arching over streams. The air starts to bristle, and paints the sky green. The leaves start to whisper their stories to me."

Gopal thought he heard the clanging of a bell, thought he heard the rubber of bicycle tires speak to the dirt on the path. Then the sounds receded into a well of silence.

Gopal no longer thought about the starting sentence to his composition. He held the pen high in his hand, and allowed the ink from above to flow into its belly.

Then, he began to write.

A Waltz Of Winged Words

As an adolescent enamored with books and literary adventures, I already was listening to "the neighing of dappled nouns,/ Soft participles coming down the steps,/ Treading on leaves, their rustling gowns..."

I was not yet familiar with Vladimir Nabokov's poetic lines quoted above, but I was no stranger to the delectations of language. I knew that a crown of words could build an empire, and a flight of well-constructed passages circle the globe's quintessence.

The English language was a festival, and the joy derived from it was interminably rich.

I read Walt Whitman's threnody on the death of Abraham Lincoln many times, drawn to it again and again by the search for a beauty whose totality seemed strangely elusive. It was as though the measure of Lincoln's greatness and the adoration of the poet could be teased out with just one more reading of "When Lilacs Last in the Dooryard Bloomed."

The flirtatious footsteps of poetry echoed in other chambers too, and there, no poet captured the imagination of language better than Dylan Thomas, Gerard Manley Hopkins, and e.e. cummings.

While childhood's gambols lasted "all the sun long," and "it was running, it was lovely" where the hay fields were "high as the house," Thomas cast a shadow on that carefree landscape with these lines: "Time held me green and dying,/ Though I sang in my chains like the sea."

I have read this poem at least a hundred times, and each time, like looking at a desert sunset, the sky of stitched words has offered me a veritable feast of colors.

It was while visiting Bradford, West Yorkshire, in 1976 to attend a wedding reception that I first heard Dylan Thomas on LP lend his voice to "Fern Hill." Over de rigueur tea and scones, and charming conversation about belles lettres, I fell in love with Thomas's poetry all over again.

On another level, with his sprung rhythm, Hopkins charmed his way into my soul with such works as "Pied Beauty," "Spring," and "The Lantern Out Of Doors."

The copy of Hopkins's book of poems that I own holds an inscription in a stranger's hand which reads: "Be full of the enthusiasm of life -- for beauty is all around."

Hopkins, more than anyone else, showed me in a handful of words "what all this juice, and all this joy" in life was about.

Another innovator of poetic language, e.e. cummings, who made words and lines break and tumble and peak as though a poem was a game of hide-and seek, captured my interest at an early age.

Is the moon "a balloon, coming out of a keen city in the sky -- filled with pretty people"? Is spring "like a perhaps hand (which comes carefully out of Nowhere) arranging a window"? Is it true that "all nearness pauses, while a star can grow"?

To look at language in a new way is to look at the world anew, and to gather in our arms, with each dappled noun and each soft participle, a more elevated measure of humanity.

In all the years that I taught school, I tried to convey to my students something of the magic of poetry, and was frequently encouraged and rewarded when they stepped gingerly into a waltz of winged words.

A Rainy Day Lesson

The new student entered the classroom unannounced and took his place in the back.

This gave rise to a buzz as my friends and I appraised and passed preliminary judgments on the newcomer, but our teacher, Mr. Bhupathi, cast a stern eye in our direction and reminded us that he would not tolerate any foolishness.

The lesson that day centered on nature poetry, and Mr. Bhupathi had latched his attention onto two lines in John Masefield's poem "Tewkesbury Road":

"O, to feel the beat of the rain, and the homely smell of the earth,
Is a tune for the blood to jig to, and joy past power of words."

These two lines were custom-made for the day at hand. My classroom was wall-less — a thatched roof supported by eight bamboo poles — and it was raining outside. I saw curtains of rain sweep across the school ground, as a gentle breeze brought the "homely smell of the earth" mingled with the aroma of jasmine.

I turned my head and looked at the newcomer. He seemed oblivious to nature and poetry in equal measure.

At the end of the lesson, Mr. Bhupathi gave us a writing assignment which required us to describe a rainy day.

The boy seated next to me raised his hand and informed our teacher that the new student had neither paper nor pencil with which to address the assignment.

"It is very kind of you to be so solicitous, but he..." Mr. Bhupathi stalled in his sarcasm, for it struck him that he did not know the new student's name.

"He is Govinda," the boy said, with a titter.

"Well, if Govinda needs a spokesman, I am certain he will let us know."

Halfway through my essay, I noticed that Govinda had managed to sneak out of the classroom. Mr. Bhupathi was sitting at his desk grading papers, and he glanced up every so often from his work to ensure that no mischief was under construction. Govinda, however, effected his exit with a timing that would have charmed a magician.

The rain had abated. In a classroom without walls, a student's mind is susceptible to diverse distractions. I tried to push them away and focus my attention on the assignment, but I was not successful. Govinda kept encroaching on my thoughts.

Why, I asked myself, would someone so insouciantly inclined toward education come to school? And why was Mr. Bhupathi, stern and exacting in his instructional habits, so lenient with Govinda? A larger question presented itself: Had Govinda become the teacher's pet?

It was at this time I noticed that my paper lunch bag was missing. I had placed it next to my school bag, and it had disappeared just as alacritously as Govinda.

Was it possible that Govinda was a thief? Had he snatched my lunch when my mind was occupied with the assignment?

I was startled out of my reverie by the sight of Govinda back in his original place.

"Did you steal my lunch?" I whispered, leaning over, and speaking under the table.

Just then Govinda stood up and grabbed the essay paper that belonged to the boy nearest to him.

"Govinda is eating my paper!" the boy exclaimed.

"Leave that goat alone," Mr. Bhupathi said, and returned to his grading.

A journey Down Mango Lane

The smell of ripe mangoes is unmistakable, inviting, and rises above the signature of all other fruits.

As soon as I walked into the grocery store, I knew the king of all fruits was there, and sure enough, a mound of mangoes sat in the middle of the produce section, an icon of supremacy.

I picked up a mango with due reverence. Most of the fruit's skin had turned a flamingo pink, and it gave slightly to my thumb's pressure; and as I raised it to my nose, the smell was replete with the promise of delectable yellow-orange flesh. I bought six mangoes for a few rupees.

Mangoes take me back a long way.

In Ernakulam, where I was living with my grandparents, there were several mango trees at the back of the house. The youngest of the lot had been planted by my great-grandmother Pattitha to commemorate my birth.

I do not know if that tree exists today, or for that matter, the house. To the left of the house was a toddy shop, and behind it a saw mill, and I suspect that one of the businesses acquired the property when my grandfather sold the house and moved with his wife to live near a temple at Guruvayoor. When he sold the house, I was living in Calcutta, and getting ready to emigrate to England.

I remember the trees fondly. They produced a bountiful harvest. I remember climbing a ladder my grandfather had built to get the fruit that hung from the lower branches. The ladder was made of bamboo poles — two long ones for the sides, with the steps made from sectional cuttings. To get the fruit way on high, my grandfather used two long bamboo poles tied together, with a sickle-like blade attached at one end. The trick was to raise the pole through the foliage to the elusive fruit, hook the stem with the blade, and give it a good, sharp yank.

My grandfather navigated the pole, while an accomplice stood nearby to catch each falling gem.

These mangoes were picked when still green, and sliced, marinated, and spiced to make hot pickles. My grandfather made mango pickles every season, and these concoctions graced all our evening meals.

Train stations in India are as busy as a Miro painting, with peddlers selling all sorts of goods, and always in the melee, one can spot a woman with a pyramid of mangoes in a wicker basket balanced on her head. It always fascinated me to watch this arrangement of fruit move like some anti-gravity device over a sea of heads.

Anywhere one travels in India, one goes by train; it is the cheapest mode of transportation. I made several trips by train, and the mangoes I tasted — Salem and Alphonso, to name just two varieties — formed an indelible impression on my mind.

Mango being the national fruit, it is ubiquitous in India. Its leaves adorn archways and doors in houses during weddings, and women wear Kanchipuram silk sarees and Kashmiri shawls with mango motifs and paisley prints on them.

So rich and delectable is the mango's stamp on my mind and palate that I have come to regard this fruit as a symbol of perfection.

An Old Man, A River, And A Few Nuggets Of Wisdom

Upon a narrow and crooked path, I met an old man whose beard was long with voyage.

"I am utterly amazed at my own prodigious ignorance," he said. "Only thusly can I acknowledge the vast sea of undiscovered knowledge into which I step every day.

"Each mind is pebble-round and star-touched, soft as feather and filled with flight.

"The light is in the eye of a man who is unafraid to walk the path alone toward some contrary truth, wherein the amethyst smiles like a child.

"In a roiling, shifting universe, the rock will fall and break the lake's mirror, shattering illusions and scattering disappointments. Each time a man thinks he has measured the light, or marked the currents where the hawk was in flight, the world moves a different mile to a different height. When the light shifts in the East from gold to black, only he who walks truth-garbed, with a tiger in his brain, will be able to overcome adversities.

"The direction of a land is the direction of a child's footsteps in the sand, and the calculations of a civilization will flounder if this truth is not allowed to stand.

"Dry words alone will not ignite the fire in the stars. The fire comes from awe, and the awe comes from God.

"It is from looking at a blade of grass that one makes the leap to ponder the mysteries of the universe. The seminal source of meaning and pulchritude in life rests in the simple events of nature: the April grand opening of a cluster of wisterias; the symphony of a mockingbird; or the darting arrows of delight in a hummingbird's gambol. Nature is God's grand museum to which we have lifelong membership.

"The world is filled with the footprints of God. Even a man who denies God acknowledges His presence by the sheer force of intellect and reasoning power with which he negates the Creator. The marvel is in every question and in every answer.

"All things that skew and cant have yet their music in the stars. So, it befits a man to move with consonance among the haphazard nature of things, and to celebrate life's differences.

"In the cathedral of the sky, full of the triumphal note of the living, a man must move like water, many-mirrored and wise.

"The earth, the tree limbs that touch the sky, and the sky itself, are felicitously wrapped in moon-paper and crayon-silk.

"Art is artlessness; innocence unsullied erudition. The songs of childhood move with prism eyes, and leap continents with little exertion. The whites of God's eyes are revealed in children's play."

Once upon a narrow and crooked path, I met a man whose beard was long with voyage. He beckoned to me, but as I approached him, he faded softly and slowly as a mist that is touched by the sun's warm fingers. In his place stood a river that stretched from my birth-cry to the present compass of my life.

In the river was a song. I picked it up, and it carried me to this place of conversation.

Fine Poetry Is A Land Of Infinite Dimensions

It was the year when the song "Don't Go Breaking My Heart" by Elton John and Kiki Dee flooded the airwaves and swept across dance floors in England. It was also the year when Steve Pizzy's mother got remarried in Bradford, West Yorkshire.

Steve, who worked with me at the Science Museum in London, was well acquainted with my passion for English literature, and since the Bronte sisters' historic home was only a short distance from his mother's residence, he invited me to the wedding.

The Writers Workshop in Calcutta, India, had just published my first book of poems, "Rings In A Tree Trunk," and I thought — and both Steve and his girlfriend agreed — that this would make an excellent wedding gift.

Our presumption was proved right. Steve's mother was delighted with the cloth-bound edition, and as if to show her appreciation, she played some LPs of Dylan Thomas reading his poems. Later that afternoon, over de rigueur tea and scones, we shared a charming conversation about belles lettres.

Steve's mother was a polymath, and what impressed me the most was the natural ease with which she quoted lines from the works of major British poets. These peregrinations from Blake to Sir John Betjeman that arched over an interesting and diverse literary landscape lent color to that day, and forever etched it in my memory.

A good poem, and indeed a great one, catches the light at many angles, and it is only through constant familiarity that the reader can hope to capture its full glow and quintessence. My teachers in India were well anchored to this tenet.

On some summer days, when a pleasant breeze traveling through curtains of rain brought the scent of jasmine and the sound of temple bells to my wall-less classroom, my teacher, Mr. Biswas, would recite a poem by Keats or Shelley from memory. His cadenced voice, mingled with the song of the rain, produced such delectable magic that the task of committing the poem to memory seemed more a gift than a chore.

I have revisited these poems many times, and each time I have discovered a new country in them, marked by a panoply of old scents and new sentiments.

"What we want is to see the child in pursuit of knowledge, not knowledge in pursuit of the child," George Bernard Shaw wrote. In the above situation, it was clearly the student who was in pursuit of words, eager to clasp them to his heart and claim ownership.

As a language arts teacher, I have always required my students to memorize selected poems, and I have always found them equal to the task.

Two years ago, I had assigned "The Road Not Taken," but, inexplicably, one student turned his attention to "Mending Wall" instead — a work of greater length and recitational complexity. Surprisingly, the student delivered the entire poem from memory with great panache the very next day.

"Of what use is it," one might ask, "to memorize a poem by Frost?"

When Michael Faraday demonstrated that a compass needle situated in proximity to a coil of wire could be moved when an electric current passed though the latter, a woman in the audience asked: "Of what use is it?"

"Well, Madam," Faraday replied, perspicaciously. "Of what use is a child?"

O! To Be Luminous And Exact

In his book-length poem "The Prodigal," Derek Walcott, winner of the 1992 Nobel Prize in literature, has his narrator cry out, "O to be luminous and exact."

Exactitude is a difficult science requiring discipline, scholarship, and perspicacity, and few people achieve it. On the other hand, the ability to be luminous requires a pure light to shine from within the soul which renders the landscape of the mind hospitable to clarity and scintillation.

Therefore, to be luminous and exact is a rich ambition for anyone to pursue.

In the hands of master wordsmiths like Walcott, Neruda, and Hopkins, language assumes a grandeur and grace, gravity and weightlessness, simplicity and intricacy that bends readers' minds to look at the world and life anew, as though miracles had transformed their vision.

Language itself is a gift from God. And just as a skilled architect aspires with his cathedral or temple to touch the heavens, the poet, with a delectation of words, builds from ordinary things magnificent edifices.

An apple a day keeps the doctor away, but a poem may accomplish more by keeping the mind free from the chains, cobwebs and doldrums of time.

A man who stops at a tree to feel its bark, and looks up to hear the soughing sounds and the notes of a mockingbird, is richer than he who passes by without acknowledging them. To be aware of the world and its seamless beauty gives purpose to life and makes better human beings of us all.

Ipso facto, this awareness needs to happen at as early an age as possible, and there is no better vehicle than poetry to bring it to fruition.

We must teach children to celebrate the grass at their feet, the clouds in the sky, and all else that lie prodigiously and delightfully between those layers.

Young people today often see the sky, but not its brindled glory; they know the artichoke, but not, what David Nelson called in the Los Angeles Times, its "succulent, secret heart hidden beneath a chevaus-de-frise of thistle-like bristle"; they hear the bird, but not the flute; they walk beside a babbling brook but don't hear its conversation with pebbles and rocks.

"Every noun," Walcott said, "has its echo."

We must teach ourselves and our children to dwell upon these echoes, and we must then be able to extract from them the quintessence of each original object.

It is easy enough to cull two or three minutes from each day toward the reading of a poem, but to appreciate its finer points demands direction and purpose that, sadly, are antithetical to today's pace of life.

However, once embarked upon, the journey of a poem is replete with rich fruits.

You Need Not Travel Far To Uncover Life's Great Truths

"Freedom is a wonderful concept, celebrated in song, speech, and literature, and idealized to have a wingspan as wide as the sky. But in real terms, how far does the river of my freedom run?" asked Grasshopper.

"You jump from country to country on the slightest provocation or whim, and should know more about freedom than I, who am so slow on my feet," answered Turtle.

"But you have so much more time to think about things. I lose my thoughts between activities, but you seem to glide along smoothly on the rails of contemplation without worry or woe. Surely you will share some of your thoughts with me."

"For a start, I am glad that you, who do not have a shell, and I, who do not have wings, have the freedom to mix our thoughts in a public place. There was a time when Flycatcher ruled this land when I was forced to spend most of my time in hiding under the ground." Turtle paused, perhaps in response to some snippet of memory that had brought pain. "I think, though," he continued after a while, "that your inquiry has less to do with external freedom and more to do with the freedom in our steps."

"That is so," said Grasshopper.

"Let me see," said Turtle. "Freedom must have purpose and vision. There is no point running helter-skelter and all over the place merely to create a drumbeat for freedom. A line segment is free to bend in a thousand places to create a purposeless abstraction, but things of beauty are gracefully curved. We can only believe in the eternity of things that are nestled in Beauty and Truth."

Grasshopper seemed to fall into a reverie. When he came out of it, he said, "I had a teacher once who told me that freedom can be a state of mind. Mahatma Gandhi was never constrained by the walls of the jails that held him captive for years. He said that rights that do not flow from duty well performed are not worth having."

"Ah," said Turtle. "Gandhi was an extraordinary man. We all cannot be like him. However, there is much truth in what you say. What good is freedom if it will not make the moonbeams dance and the stars sing? With or without freedom, whether wearing a crown or ragged clothes, we all shall be dust one day. Only the good work that we do and the love that we raise will stand us in good stead."

"Is it not true," asked Grasshopper, "that our journeys in search of things and meaning carry us more miles than we need to go? The same teacher who talked to me about freedom told me that the entire universe is visible and ready for embrace from right where we stand."

"We travel extensively when we look closely at things that are near at hand. There are rings in a tree trunk, my friend, and a simple pebble carries a tome of history. There are those who think that my slow locomotive power is a shortcoming, but really, I have crossed continents on a patch of grass."

"What is the difference between the young and the old?" Grasshopper asked.

"A great painter once said that it takes a lot of years to become young. Aging is a process by which we lose a lot to regain what we already had. Old age is the recognition that there is great velocity in stillness."

"I will go now," said Grasshopper, "but between hops I will remember the things you said. I will look in familiar places for unfamiliar things, and should a moment speak some new truth, I will give it my ear."

Other Books by Ramnath Subramanian

The Jasmine House of Ernakulam (a novel)
ISBN: 978-1300388180

In the bustling town of Mala Nagar, India, the miracles of the holy man on Prayer Hill continue to weave their magic, touching lives in unexpected and extraordinary ways. Once a destitute beggar, Qabila has grown into a spirited young woman under the nurturing care of Linda Stevens, and is now a celebrated movie star. She uses her celebrity status to bring attention to the plight of homeless children and along the way meets and falls in love with Roger Fletcher—the son of a Texas oil tycoon. Guided by the unseen hand of the holy man, Qabila and Roger overcome societal and geographical barriers to form a union that is a testament to true love. Funny, tender, and wrapped in the rich fabric of Indian culture, The Jasmine House of Ernakulam offers a window into the charms of Indian life and points to the profound depths of religion and philosophy that underscore it. This is the fifth in the Holy Man series of novels.

A Miracle of Cranes (a novel)
ISBN: 978-1304590787

Mala Nagar came into prominence when a holy man moved into a burned-out house on Prayer Hill and started performing miracles. Among the steady stream of visitors to this town was Kenneth Fletcher—an oil tycoon from Texas— who wanted to get a picture taken with the holy man to impress his business associates back home. Little did he know when he made the trip that he himself would become a participant in one of the miracles. His friendship with Linda Raman and her family—who have close ties to the holy man—and the vision he has on Prayer Hill with a visitation of cranes, lead him on a path to found the Ernakulam Children's Project, just as a vision of swans circling overhead caused Sibelius to write his famous Fifth Symphony. This, the fourth book in the Holy Man series, shows how compassion, caring, and direct action can make a transformative difference in the lives of needy, lost, and dispossessed children. Funny, poignant, and richly clothed in humanity, the story presents a charming picture of Indian life and Indian culture.

Qabila Finds A Home (a novel)
ISBN: 978-1365500541

Linda Stevens came to Mala Nagar, India, to do research on the potters and clay-makers of that region. During her stay, the town is cast into national prominence because a holy man, who has taken up residence in an abandoned, burned-out house on Prayer Hill, starts performing miracles. Soon, with the guiding hand of the holy man orchestrating events, Linda assumes the role of a foster mother and becomes the central force in the lives of a young orphan boy named Gopal, and a homeless beggar girl named Qabila. Through an extraordinary catenation of events, -all inside the patchwork of miracles, -Linda becomes the manager of the Miracle of the Rose Children's Center. This, the third book in a trilogy, shows how compassion, caring, and direct action can make a transformative difference in the lives of needy, lost, and dispossessed children. Funny, poignant, and richly clothed in humanity, the story presents a charming picture of Indian life and Indian culture.

Miracle of the Rose (a novel)
ISBN 978-1387504923

"I'm amazed at how everything in life circles back to its origin to make a new beginning," said Savitri. "Consider these circularities: A street-smart kid named Gopal connects with a holy man who has moved into a burned-out house on Prayer Hill, and helps him perform two miracles; Linda connects with Gopal; the holy man then uses Gopal to connect Linda with Raman and Kumortuli; a train journey to Calcutta to visit Kumortuli connects Linda with my husband; and now, there is the connection to the bookseller's daughter. The center of all these circles, of course, is Mala Nagar. I think we'll soon find out what the new circles are." When will the holy man return to Prayer Hill, and will there be new miracles? What new paths will Linda Steven's life take, and what role will Raman and Gopal play in these transformations? The story offers a window into the charms of Indian life, and points to the profound depths of religion and philosophy that underscore it. This is the second in a trilogy of novels.

The House on Prayer Hill (a novel)
ISBN 978-1387695188

After suffering two divorces and realizing that she was a poor judge of men, Linda Stevens decides to pursue a degree in anthropology. The research project she selects,—Pottery and Image Makers of India,—lands her in the town of Mala Nagar, where a holy man and a 10-year-old boy named Gopal enter the circle of her life. The holy man who has taken residence in a burned-out house on Prayer Hill, performs two miracles,—almost reluctantly,—that put the town on the regional map. Linda also befriends the filmmaker Venkat Raman, who decides to produce a documentary about the happenings on Prayer Hill. The holy man talks to Gopal and no one else, and has him participate in the miracles, which make the young boy everyone's darling in town. While capturing the special bond that exists between the holy man and Gopal, and between "Memsahib" Linda and Gopal, the story offers a window into the charms of Indian life, and points to the profound depths of religion and philosophy that underscore it. This is the first in a trilogy of novels.

Zeek the Photographer (a novel)
ISBN 978-1716253881

Susan Murphy cannot walk away from her failed marriage because the memory of her husband, Zeek, saving her from a burning building keeps getting in the way. Instead, she puts in for a job transfer and gets assigned to the Madolina retail chain store in Florence, Italy. There she meets Antonio Corelli and finds new beginnings. Meanwhile, Zeek quits his teaching job and takes up photography as a profession, encouraged and inspired by Bridgit Muller, whom he meets by happenstance while taking a walk along the Rhine. Bridgit's rise to stardom as Zeek's model is a story of love, betrayal, and growth, set mostly in Rome, Florence, Venice, and London.

Bridgit the Model (a novel)
ISBN 978-1008942974

After suffering an unexpected betrayal by her photographer companion and lover, the media-savvy and much celebrated model, Bridgit, whose sensuous poses are displayed on billboards all across Europe, attempts to put her life back together. Chance encounters with a lost dog and a boy whom she befriended in an alley in Rome, act as catalysts for the "Mona Lisa of Advertising" to embark on a new path, while still pursuing fame. The story set sumptuously in Rome and Florence, filled with literary and artistic allusions, and powered by love, is one of transformation, transcendence, and triumph.

A Touch Of Miracle (a novella)
ISBN 978-1105032745

Sanjay, an orphan, who is living in Calcutta with his grandmother, has dropped out of college to write a novel. The temple town of Guruvayoor is the setting for his novel, and in the story it becomes a sanctuary for a young girl named Rani who has run away from home to avoid an unwanted marriage. A series of miracles at the temple reorient Rani's life and strengthen her faith. As Sanjay is penning a story filled with miracles, he cannot account for some of the chapters he has written. Even though they are in his handwriting, he cannot remember ever writing them. His friend, Radhika, helps him in his literary pursuit and offers moral support. Together they tackle the mystery surrounding them and become the beneficiaries of small miracles themselves.

A Second Meeting (a novella)
ISBN 978-1312447462

Kenneth, a successful businessman, whose wife died 19 years ago when she was just 23 years old, lives with memories of her, holding on to the philosophy that in one lifetime you can truly and fully love only one person. But what if life and death have dimensions and realities that are beyond our understanding? A series of discoveries, — many of them involving Susanna, a recently hired kitchen help who happens to be a prodigy with the piano—force Kenneth to rethink his philosophy and to reorient his life. While serendipity and happenstance play their hand, Amira, a piano coach to Susanna, seems to have the measure of the mysteries that are swirling around in the household.

A Sprinkling Of Pixie Dust: Essays on Education and Classroom Practices
ISBN 978-1716116117

What lessons do green-haired boys teach us? What misadventures happen when a teacher allows his students to chase an invisible rabbit in search of a story? Can you have a boredom factor of 4, and still be successful in school? Is the crown on the king's head what the spider saw? These and other ideas are explored in this collection of essays culled from my newspaper columns published in the El Paso Times between 1998 and 2019.

Arrow and A Song: Essays on Language, Fine Arts, and Travel
ISBN 978-1716266539

Language should march with vigor and move like a minuet. Great art can melt away the world, and a great symphony can make the world stand still. Travel can take one to serendipity's stations. These and other ideas are explored in this collection of essays culled from my newspaper columns published in the El Paso Times between 1998 and 2019.

Feathers 1,2,3: Essays on Nature and Animals
ISBN 978-1716231384

Welcome to the pyramid of the rose, the Danube of the wisteria, the towering peak of the ocotillo. Welcome, also, to the Taj Mahal of the peacock, the royal barge of the grackle, and the temple of the caparisoned elephant. These and other delectations from nature are explored in this collection of essays culled from my newspaper columns published in the El Paso Times between 1998 and 2019.

A Melody Of Flying Flutes: Essays On People, Places, And Things, Remembered
ISBN 978-1716199240

I am happy when I see atoms dance. I like the conversation of strangers in new places. I like turning the pages of books, and going on new journeys to new places. I like to hear the whistle of a train leaving a platform, nudging the compass needle to a new resting place. I like the sound of a ship's horn announcing a departure to a new destination. The sun shines with vigor. The river sings joyously. All is gold and blessed. These and other ideas are explored in this collection of essays culled from my newspaper columns published in the El Paso Times between 1998 and 2019.

The Message In The Rain: An otherworldly love story
ISBN 978-1716064807

A bereaved husband chases after the memories of his wife in a war-torn country, and receives signs and messages that point to a reunion on the 'other side.' Ian's path intersects with those of a few people — enigmas themselves — who help to shed light on the mysteries embedded in the messages.

Prisms and Bells: A collection of poems
ISBN 978-1716185922

The knowledge of the sun that is young once only inspires us to bring wings and passion to all the things we wish to accomplish in life. At the heart of poetry is a desire to make language sing a different song than has been heard before. When and where it succeeds, poetry offers a new country on the map that is full of delectations.

The Bridge to Bridgit
ISBN 978-1387924219

Famed and celebrated European model, Bridgit Muller, dubbed the Mona Lisa of Advertising, has set forth in this book her thoughts on a wide variety of subjects. Combining graceful language and a poetic idiom, these colorful and robust excursions into the realm of personal truths reveal a sensitive soul that is keenly aware that life is more than billboards and magazine covers splashed with sensuous poses. People who read this book — especially those who are familiar with Bridgit's triumphs in the fashion world — will be amazed at the depth and perspicacity she brings to the commonplace and complex aspects of the world at large.

Sticky Wicket and Other Vexations
ISBN 978-1387924219

Brian Cleary was among a handful of workers who still wore a purple tie to work. He eschewed the red tie, as he did the Brain Tonic which was reputed to increase productivity at work, because he was suspicious about both of them. But how long can he abide the pressures building up around him to conform to his milieu? What will he do and how will things turn out? There are other vexations in the world that are real rather than fictional, and I had addressed them in several of my weekly newspaper columns published in the El Paso Times between 1998 and 2019. Here, the dystopian story and a selection of my newspaper columns set up a sticky wicket for our times, and offer a panoply of ideas for reflections and resolution.

The Bus To Agra (a novel)
ISBN: 978-1716140785

After finding out that her fiancé has been cheating on her, Jennifer Blaise runs away to India to seek a new direction in her life. On her flight to New Delhi, she meets widower, Kiran Patel, who invites her to stay with his family in Nana Nagar until she is able to find proper accommodations. Jennifer becomes fast friends with Kiran's daughter-in-law, Radha, and is drawn to a homeless boy named Nanda. When she tries to enroll Nanda in school, she meets an independent journalist, Jai Jaiprakash, who becomes an important part of her life. Jai is shy when it comes to matters of the heart, and Jennifer has tossed romance aside after being jilted in love. Will the bus trip to Agra change things? What role will Nanda's "mandir" rock, which he gives to Jennifer as a talisman, play in the outcome of events? Life in India——-with all its eccentricities, charms, and wisdom—comes to life in this endearing West-meets-East love story.

The Sariwallah (a novel)
ISBN: 978-1458390424

Rachel Flynn came to India to gather material for her second novel. She settled happily in a charming town full of friendly people, -that is, until the anonymous notes started to arrive. "If you know what's good for you, you'll stay away from the American woman. If you don't heed this warning, things will get very nasty for you," warned the first note, sent to a school master who had brought Rachel as a guest speaker to his classroom. As Police Chief Motilal proceeds with his investigation and starts connecting the dots, he discovers that there's more to the notes than meets the eye. Who is writing the notes? What is the hidden motive behind them? Will Motilal uncover the plot before something serious happens? Along the way as the story unfolds, the reader is treated to some colorful characters and the infinite charms of Indian life.

Journey To A Second Spring (a novel)
ISBN: 978-1435780477

For five years, Jake Johns made a living playing the stock market. He then started to dabble in craps at a Las Vegas casino, because he found comfort in mathematics and a sureness in numbers- elements which were missing in his 12-year marriage. During one of his gaming sessions at Drake's Diamond Casino, he encounters Holly Simmons, who makes big bets and has a unique and reckless way of throwing the dice. Attracted to the "heretic shooter," first by her play and then by the obtuseness of her personality, he manages to forge a friendship which makes him reevaluate his marriage and his life's goals. Will he come out richer or poorer, smarter or foolish, from his new dalliance with gambling and a mystery woman? Holly soon becomes a Las Vegas celebrity because of her shooting style and the enormous success she enjoys at the craps table. She shoots with her eyes closed, and is often seen talking to herself before throwing the dice. People are convinced that there is an outside force that is guiding her hand. Who is Holly, the reclusive resident at the casino's hotel, and what is the story of her life? Craps aficionados will enjoy this story as much as romantics, who believe in the eternal and otherworldly aspects of true love.

The Flower Girl of Panipat (a novel)
ISBN: 978-1387873449

Two crossword clues had something to do with Jim Driscoll going to Panipat, India, to be a resident at the Neela Akash Writers' Retreat. Once there, a flower girl— who first appeared to him in a dream, and then in real life (are they the same person?)—takes him on a journey of serendipitous discoveries. While staying at the retreat, widower Jim is drawn to the charms of Indian author Kamala Sharma, whose singsong voice makes him a prisoner so as to make the world disappear outside her circumference. Both are fascinated by the identity of the flower girl and the mysterious way in which she injects herself into Jim's life. In her final manifestation, the flower girl performs a miracle that changes the lives of Jim and Kamala forever. The story captures the delightfulness and appeal of Indian life, while at the same time pointing to the profound depths of religion and philosophy that inform and underscore it.

Talkative Man Talks…and other conversations
ISBN: 978-1387810826

During the course of writing a weekly newspaper column for the El Paso Times for 20 years, I invented several characters—Talkative Man, The Whip, the Mayor of Trance Town, among them —whose conversations and interactions provided a useful vehicle for carrying certain ideas forward. I took this approach in the belief that satirical, verbal exchanges between colorful characters in whimsical settings—such as, the Loose Marbles School District—can expose the cracks in human nature and political systems with greater economy and alacrity than regular prose. In the vignettes included in this collection, a removal of the disguise of nonsense and flamboyancy offers a window through which the real world comes into view, replete with contradictions, corruptions, and celebrations.

www.ingramcontent.com/pod-product-compliance
Lightning Source LLC
Chambersburg PA
CBHW081600270726
48657CB00029B/3401